Women of Valour Series IX

"Double Grace"

Dr. Allison Wiley and WOV Contributors

Women of Valour Series IX

"*Double Grace*"
*Dr. Allison Wiley
& WOV Contributors*

Copyright © 2025

All rights reserved. No part of this publication may be reproduced, stored in a retrieval system, or transmitted in any form by any means, for example, electronic, photocopy, recording, scanning, or other without prior written permission of the publisher. The only exception is brief quotations in printed reviews.

CONTENTS

January..Page 5
Dr. Allison Wiley
Prophetess Hope McDowell- Gibson

February..Page 19
Shekanah Hill-Tetteh

March..Page 36
Janell Williams

April..Page 44
Hannah Jones

May...Page 54
Wendy Dangerfield- Jones

June..Page 70
Helen Miller

July...Page 80
Prudence Oppong

August..Page 86
Michelle Cardwell

September......................................Page 94
Alysa Elliott- Wilson

October..Page 106
Ashley Baxter

November......................................Page 121
Mellonie Baldwin

December......................................Page 136
Brunell Johnson

January

Dr. Allison Wiley

Meet Dr. Allison Wiley

Dr. Allison Wiley is the Founder of Women of Valour, a mandate prophetically spoken into her life in 2016. GOD has called Dr. Wiley to inspire women to fight life's battles by standing firmly on The Promises of GOD.

Dr. Wiley believes Women of Valour will be a catalyst for revival in The Kingdom of GOD. She is an ordained Evangelist and the author of LIFTED.

Shoot The Arrow

"And he said, "Open the window eastward." And he opened it. Then Elisha said, "Shoot." And he shot. And he said, "The arrow of the Lord's deliverance and the arrow of deliverance from Syria, for thou shalt smite the Syrians in Aphek till thou have consumed them." -2 Kings 13:17

2 Kings 13 tells the story of Prophet Elisha and Israel's King . Before Elisha dies, he does one last great thing for Israel He joins hands with its ruler to shoot an arrow at Syria through an open window. Elisha proclaims it The Lord's arrow of deliverance. Yes! The arrow of deliverance against Israel's nemesis and formidable enemy-Syria.

In Elisha's time, Syria was known for crossing Israel's borders to commit heinous crimes of exploitation. But when The Lord's Arrow was released, Israel defeated Syria in Aphek.
WOW!! VICTORY

The year 2025 is such a window. A window called Grace. The deliverance arrow is heading straight for the enemy. The areas where we failed, we'll "shoot arrows" from places of prayer supported by organized movements.

This grace is not just about favor but it's grace to target the enemy in spaces, places, and areas he crept in and invaded. The best results in advancing The Church will be yielded through grace and deliverance.

I've got an arrow!

And if you think about it. so do you!

Who's ready to SHOOT and take the enemy down????

Let The Church Rise

"Elisha had become sick with the illness of which he would die. Then Joash the king of Israel came down to him, and wept over his face, and said, "O my father, my father, the chariots of Israel and their horsemen!" **- 2 Kings 13:14**

Elisha had become sick with the illness of which he would die. Then Joash the king of Israel came down to him, and wept over his face, and said, "O my father, my father, the chariots of Israel and their horsemen!"

This passage of scripture helps us understand we must fight when the need arises.

Elisha was old and dying but yet he released The Lord's Arrow. It's never too late to shoot your shot! You're never too old to fight for The Church.

King Joash was weeping. Grieving his prophet's imminent transition. But he pulled back the bow and took the shot. Even on your worst day, you can still give GOD your best fight

It's never about convenience. It's about seizing moments. 2025 is a window of opportunities. But without prayer, faith, and action, the window can close.

Don't talk yourself out of DOUBLE GRACE AND DELIVERANCE. GOD'S window is open for you.

Seize grace in 2025!

Release deliverance in 2025!

Don't live in the enemy's plans in 2025!

Help THE CHURCH rise to the occasion in 2025!

TAKE THE SHOT IN 2025!

January

Prophetess Hope McDowell-Gibson

Meet Prophetess Hope McDowell-Gibson

Her Excellency Rev Dr the Honorable Hope McDowell-Gibson, OEA, Th.D, Ph.D.

Prophetess, Revivalist, Senior Pastor, Co-Founder of No Limits Ministries International, Founder & President of HANS TV Network. Dr Hope has purposed to encourage and provide development of creative Leadership to the Body of Christ. Through her Leadership Trainings, Prophetic Mentorship Programs and HANS School Of The Prophets.

Prophetess Hope is a Conference and Motivational Speaker successfully been in the business world for many years and is a seasoned executive coach. She has purposed to train and equip Fivefold Leaders to work in advancing and establishing the Kingdom of God.

Prophetess, is a strong prophetic voice and an End time Prophet, her Ministry is followed by notable signs, wonders and miracles. She is the Author of three books; THE PERSON OF THE HOLY SPIRIT IN YOU, NONE SHALL LACK THEIR MATE and 100% GUARANTEED ANSWERS TO YOUR PRAYERS.

A Greater Grace Is Needed!

The early church was faced with persecution and backlash as they preached Jesus in Jerusalem. Amidst this, as they gathered from house to house to pray and fellowship "Great Grace" was multiplied upon them for Mighty Signs & Wonders.

Like the early church as depicted in the book of Acts, which functioned according to the Fivefold Ministry model, it is crucial for the End Time church to be restored and reformed to align with its original purpose. As spoken by Peter in Acts 3:21 saying; "Jesus whom the heaven must receive until the time for restoring all the things about which God spoke by the mouth of his holy prophets long ago." emphasizes the importance of this transformative process.

Consequently, the practical approach to Fivefold Ministry adoption is critical. In other words, they must be restored back to the church. Jesus expects the Body of Christ to function in the earth as He did. It is impossible for the "End Time" church to be fully grown up to our destiny without the input and contribution of the Fivefold Ministry Office, which is the maturity mechanism of the church.

This is Spiritual Maturation!

The scripture tells us that each office is given a measure of Grace; the number five is the number that represents Grace. Only when the Fivefold ascension gifts is operating together, we will experience the full manifestation of the Power of God in completeness.

The Fivefold ministry gifts, as outlined in scripture, include Apostles, Prophets, Evangelists, Pastors, and Teachers. They represent the measure of the grace of God being demonstrated on the Earth; Acts 4:33 says with Great Power the Apostles witnessed to the resurrection of the Lord Jesus Christ, and great grace was upon them all.

Grace is not just unmerited favour, but it means the enabling Power of God that will enable you to do what He has called you to do. For this reason, Apostle Paul says, I am what I am by the Grace of God. Again, the scripture mentioned that there was great grace upon the church in Jerusalem. It was great power that the apostles witness to the resurrection of the Lord Jesus Christ.

The full measure of God's grace was released in the early church. So much so, that the church was so Powerful. They were experiencing the full measure of God's grace, and they were releasing it to the world. For example, Apostles are graced with a "Powerful Anointing" to go into a region and bring the Kingdom of God.

Let's embrace this Fivefold Ministry Grace to experience mighty miracles and deliverance in 2025 and beyond!

The Dimension of Grace!

James reveals that God gives more Grace. The phrase "But He gives us more grace" introduces a profound theological truth about God's character and His relationship with humanity.

The Greek word for "grace" is "charis," which signifies unmerited favour and divine assistance given to humans for their regeneration and sanctification. In the context of James, this grace is not static but dynamic, continually offered to believers to empower them to overcome challenges and live in accordance with God's will.

Essentially, God's grace is abundant and sufficient to meet every need. God's grace is abundant and available, but it requires a posture of humility to receive it. Recognize that grace is not earned but given to those who acknowledge their need for God.

God Gives More Grace to the Humble.

The phrase "but gives grace to the humble" completes the contrast between the proud and the humble.

The humble denotes someone who is lowliness of mind and a recognition of one's dependence on God.

In the biblical context, humility is fundamentally about recognizing our own limitations and the essential need for God's guidance and grace. It is not merely a reflection of feelings of inadequacy or low self-worth; rather, true humility involves a conscious acknowledgment of our dependence on God. This mindset aligns with the teachings of Scripture, which encourage us to submit to God's authority and rely on His wisdom.

When we embrace this form of humility, we create an open channel for God's grace to flow into our lives. This grace is transformative; it empowers believers to overcome their shortcomings, resist temptation, and embody the moral and ethical standards that God desires for us. By understanding our need for divine assistance, we become more receptive to the Holy Spirit's work within us, enabling us to live righteously and fulfill His will and purposes in our lives.

February

Shekanah Hill-Tetteh

Meet Shekanah Hill-Tetteh

Shekanah J Hill-Tetteh (Shekanah Joy) is a servant of God. Shekanah is a woman of power and passion. She is a certified life coach, Certified Christian Counselor, Author and Ordained Crisis Chaplain. Shekanah is the daughter of late Apostle/ Pastor Stephen Oliver Hill Sr. and Vivian Hill. Shekanah Hill- Tetteh is a devoted wife to George Tetteh (Tettey) and a wonderful mom to Zion Hill. She is currently expecting the gift of life that the Lord has blessed her womb with to carry in the earth realm that is due in the latter middle of 2025. She is an anointed apostolic/prophetic intercessor, prophet of the lord's church and also a teachable emerging apostolic voice. She is a graduate of Phoenix Arizona with a bachelor's in business management and CHRM (certificate in Human Resource). Shekanah has completed her master's in business with an emphasis in Health Administration. She is currently

At a young age, Yahweh's hand was upon

Shekanah life. At a young age 6, Shekanah would dream and prophesy. Shekanah was prophesied to of the great calling of God on her life again at the age 8 and ongoing into adulthood. Shekanah always had a heart for God and to serve. She faithfully served on many auxiliaries because she understood servitude. Shekanah preached her first sermon at the age of 17 under the tutelage of Pastor Gerald T. Miller and lady Diane Miller of Elyton Missionary Baptist Church, Under the direction of Youth director Janine Parham. Shekanah served as a youth advisor and led many congregational prayer calls.

Shekanah acknowledged the call on her life for many years but didn't fully embrace the title until late 2018. In 2018, Dr. Bridget Israel was one of the first one to lay hands in Houston concerning my prophetic call. In May of 2019, Prophetess Kendria Moore came to Houston at the church she attended. She prophesied to Shekanah the word of the Lord. Many other prophetic and apostolic voices anointed Shekanah throughout late 2019.In June 2021, the lord spoke and said you are not just a prophet but are my apostolic gift to the body of Christ. Many leaders have prophesied since then. You operate and function in some magnitude before it is recognized.

In March of 2020, Shekanah was invited by prophetess Kendria Moore as a guest on her TV broadcasting show called prophetic impact (WATC-TV57) in Atlanta Georgia. She has been on Women's Thursday (Worldwide Gospel Connection), where Apostle Kisshima is the Host frequently. Shekanah mission is empowering women, inspiring and encourage women. Shekanah has also been on other platforms spreading the gospel. She is the Kingdom Enforcer, that enforces the principles of God, precepts, edicts and kingdom foundation.

Shekanah has always been devoted to prayer but has intensified her sword of the spirit through the secret place and much endurance. Shekanah is an Apostolic-prophetic Intercessor that is called to shake the foundation of hell. This great burden for prayer was birthed through much pain. Her heart desire is to see God move on behalf of his people. Shekanah is the founder of Shekanah Joy Ministries. She is also the founder of The Birthing Prayer Chambers; Women of prestige Arise conference and Extending a Helping Hand Outreach (non-profit). This non-profit organization is a burden on her heart to help those that are less fortunate to find temporary housing and resources needed to shift their lives. Mrs. Hill-Tetteh is also working on her 501c3, and her women independent living facility alongside fulfilling the needs of the group home. Shekanah Hill-Tetteh is also the owner of "Be thou Restored Counseling and Coaching Services. She is the author of "No more cycles, From Rejection & Brokenness, Now Victorious" and is currently working on next project, called My shoes have changed. Shekanah is currently working on a workbook and course that will launch in detail in late 2025. Shekanah is currently working on a woman's course for all women to understand their priestly anointing and how to govern their authority. Many people don't understand who they are because they want to fill shoes that they never meant to fill because of trauma and rejection but the Lord has come to set the captives free. Break the chain of false labels, false titles, to identify that you are enough. She has done many broadcasts on identity and will continue for the forward movement of the church. She is working on her course for intercessors to be fillers/interceptors of the gap and restore the Lord's altar. Shekanah's passion for God wants to see women and men free and doing all that God has called them to do in the earth realm. The word of God tells us to occupy. The Greek word translated "occupy" in our King James Version is "pragmateuomai" which means "to busy oneself" doing all that God has called them to do in the earth realm. Shekanah is a change agent in her generation that draws those to one agenda, to fulfill kingdom and a passion for Christ. She is a Kingdom enforcer of her generation.

Shekanah Hill-Tetteh's greatest desire is to honor God with her whole life. Shekanah believes that her assignment is to encourage people of all walks of life to stay postured in God and knowing that God cannot fail. She has a hunger and passion to restore the original intent of the church and bring apostolic order in the lord's church but the leading of the Chief commander Jesus Christ. She is led to the lost, rejected, oppressed, broken, and suppressed but that is not her only assignment. I am a weeping prophet because we have the power through Christ Jesus to destroy what is trying to overtake us. We the ecclesia shall arise with great power and shall be victorious. No matter what they're going through, Shekanah believes the trial won't break you but will make you fit for your prestigious priestly assignment.

Deliverers ARISE!!!!

The Deliverers will not look like what you are acquainted with seeing but will have the scent of the father. They will be an assistance to your next. Hear the clarion call from on high. ARISE and sit in heavenly places.

Exodus 3

The father said he is raising up delivers, re-strategizing his deliverers, shaking the dust off them, retraining them and releasing them into the land. That they will be an assistance to speak life and deposit the newness, as it will reflect the King's glory. There is a window where we must take territory. Go in bold and without fear. The Kingdom will advance. HA!!! Rise to be a full extension of the father. To be the beacon of light and to walk with sword against darkness. They have been on the backside of the mountain, in the low valley, walking with one with father, eating and drinking from the bitter cup.

I Prophecy that you will no longer be bound to old system, that you are walking in the favor of the Lord, walking into the grace of the Lord. I speak to every old and expired cycle. I come against everything that has held you back from walking in the fullness of who the father has called you to be. I break the fallow ground from the tattered soil, tattered foundation, to bring forth the new. I speak the everything that father has engraved upon your very existence will usher you into your internal expected end. That the PNUEMA of God will blow upon the dry bones. I speak that the wisdom of the ancient of days goes with you. I speak now that the DNA coded in your very sequence of identity will break forth as you grow in weight, height, depth and transform, transfigure into the fullness of who you are. I speak as a vessel, the creed on behalf of the Kingdom of heaven.

We can see throughout scripture, when the father wanted to raise someone up to be a person that will break the systems of old and bring deliverance to a nation or region, he will first take you through deliverance. Moses became a delivered because he was first delivered from an old system and way of living. He will allow you to see what you are called to and change you to be fit for the assignment. He will bring you through growth and evolution. The father will call you to the fire. You must be delivered from old mindsets, old strategies, old foundation. The father will call you to offset, to disrupt, overthrow, eradicate, to pioneer, to forerun, to be a carrier, to lead, and to run the race well. Your cup of suffering is a bitter drink. You must walk in the valley low, desert dry, the heat of the furnace. The father will purify your vessel. They have been impacted, infused, activated with power of the KAVOD of God. The redemptive expression of the father. You will feel it first before you have experienced it. Before you become a deliverer, you must feel it. God will raise up a deliverer up because he has smelled the deceit of the nations, he has seen the despair of his people, he has heard the unjust in the land.

The father will make you a battle axe in his hand. He will cause you to be a sharpened soldier because you will get your marching orders from headquarters. The soldiers must be taught by their father how to hear, see, be skillful and be a demonstration in the land. The father has predestined, scribed, engraved your destiny. Your father has handpicked you to become the beacon of light, and you must walk it out to the fullest because there are people that need your gifting, administration, and the strategy of heaven through you. Where the father will have you to go as your feet touch the earth walking in the fullness of the authority of the one who has sent you. You will understand the originality of who father has called you to be making indentions in the earth. You will bring forth what glorifies Kingdom in every dimension of your life and help usher in the divine reset that leads to revival.

We must first understand that the DELIVERER is He that has sent you, sanctioned you and called you. Exodus 3:14 "I AM WHO I AM. This is what you are to say to the Israelites: 'I HAVE sent me to you.'" Deliverers I want to urge you to know that you are sent as a representation of the expression of the father but know it is the spirit of the Lord who has graced you. Not by your power nor your own might. You are not THE deliverer in your own doing but a representation of the one that has sent you. Watch who you shun away because of what you thought they should be, but they come with orders and the backing of heaven.

Arise from the ashes, arise from the burning bush, arise with your arrows and your sword, strike the rock, ARISE with your marching orders from headquarters. Selah! AGAIN, I say Selah!!

Look Ahead to Where You Are Going!!!!

The Hebrew word for "forward" is "קדימה) "pronounced kadimah). It conveys the idea of moving forward, advancing, or progressing.
Philippians 3:13-14 Brethren, I count not myself to have apprehended: but this one thing I do, forgetting those things which are behind, and reaching forth unto those things which are before, 14 I press toward the mark for the prize of the high calling of God in Christ Jesus.

Proverbs 4:25 Let your eyes look directly forward, and your gaze be straight before you. When you are driving the main focal point is to look ahead where you are going. To look forward to the destination where you are going.

Yes, you may look over in your mirror as you transition through lanes, but you cannot be distracted at what is behind you!!!! Looking back could also signify being distracted or not fully focused on God's purpose.

In Philippians 3:13-14 we can see that Apostle Paul expresses his commitment to pressing forward in his faith journey, despite past struggles, failures, or achievements. Paul emphasizes the importance of letting go of past mistakes, regrets, or even past successes. Clinging to the past can hinder spiritual growth. He encourages believers to focus on the future and the mission that God has ahead for them. Watch this, Apostle Paul speaks about actively striving towards the goal of spiritual maturity and the ultimate reward of eternal life with God. Apostle Paul himself, despite being an apostle and having had many spiritual experiences, emphasizes that he has not yet "arrived" or "reached perfection." Instead, he is still striving toward the goal.

Apostle Paul emphasizes that pressing on toward the goal in Christ, we must keep our eyes fixed on Him. Jesus is the "author and perfecter of our faith" (Hebrews 12:2), and by focusing on Him, we are equipped to overcome obstacles and grow in grace. You are called to GREATER!!!

God's best is often found in forward movement because, as Scripture teaches, God's plan for His people is one of growth, progress, and transformation. Moving forward in faith, obedience, and trust in God allows us to fully embrace the promises and blessings he has for us.

It's PROGRESSIVE!!!

Our best is tied to moving toward the future, trusting that God's promises will come to pass. Our best in the forward movement SOLDIERS!!!! God best in the forward movement, NOT behind you.

We can also see this in Genesis 19:17-26. God warns Lot and his family to flee from the city of Sodom, which was about to be destroyed because of its wickedness. They are told not to look back as they escape. In verse 26, Lot's wife looks back at the burning city of Sodom despite the warning, and as a result, she turns into a pillar of salt. The pillar of salt symbolizes the
consequences of clinging to the past, especially when it keeps us from moving

forward in faith. Lot's wife looked back, longing for the comfort or familiarity of Sodom, even though God was
leading her to a better future.

DECLARATION: I decree today that we will move forward in faith, leaving behind all that is in the past. I declare that we will no longer be held back by the regrets of yesterday or the distractions of the past. We shall choose to focus on the future that God has for us, and we walk in the direction He has set before me. I declare that we are pressing on toward the goal of Christlikeness, embracing the transformation that God is working in me. We shall trust that His promises for my life are yes and amen, and we believe that His best is ahead of us. I decree and declare that we shall not shrink back in fear or uncertainty, but we will move forward with courage, knowing that God is with me every step of the way. I declare and declare that we are empowered by the Holy Spirit to overcome every obstacle, to rise above every challenge, and to claim every blessing that God has prepared for us .I decree and declare that the best days are ahead of us and we shall step into the fullness of God's purpose and destiny for our life. I decree that we will grow, we will prosper, and we will fulfill the calling He has placed on our lives. Amen.

March

Janell Williams

Meet Janell Williams

Janell Williams was baptized in Jesus Name and received the gift of the Holy Ghost under the Pastorate of District Elder Willie E. Gibson in 1969. In the year of 1982, she was called into the ministry. It wasn't until 1983 when she preached her first sermon under the leadership of Bishop Clarence Stewart Jr. who was a District Elder at the time. She served in various areas of the Ministry.

Later, she enlisted into the U.S. Marine Corps and move away from Texas. While living in Sigonella, Italy, she served on the ministerial staff at the Navy Chapel. She taught Bible Study and preached in homes and in the Chapel. She was one of the ministers who established the first ever United Pentecostal service held in the Chapel on a military base. Bishop Michael Franklin, who was the District Elder over the European District at the time, anointed and mentored her and the other ministers for the work of the Lord in Sigonella, Italy. She served on the ministerial staff and as President of the Women's Ministry at the Navy Chapel. She received her licensed as an Evangelist by the Pentecostal Assemblies of the World, Inc. while serving in the Navy Chapel in Okinawa, Japan.

She returned home to Texas in 2002. Currently she serves on the Ministerial staff, a Teacher, an Altar Worker and on the Board of Trustees under the leadership of Bishop Titus B. Stewart. Previously she served as an Under-shepherd and Altar Workers Director. In 2024, she received training under the Apostolic Development of Prophets School and was elevated to the Office of Prophet. February 25, 2025, she received her Certification in the 5-Fold Ministry Academy from Impact University (John Eckhardt Founder). Aside from her regular duties at work, she is a Chaplain.

Janell Williams is a grateful mother of three children and five grandchildren. In her spare times, she enjoys writing, reading, singing and traveling.

The Pour

"And other sheep I have, which are not of this fold: them also I must bring, and they shall hear my voice; and there shall be one fold, and one shepherd." -John 10:16

I'm pouring into My people.

Those who love the Most High God, I have enlarged their capacity to receive the pour. This pour is greater than they have ever experienced. It will not leak out. It will not waste. Because when I pour My precious oil, My precious anointing, they will walk in discernment. They will not waste the oil. And as they pour out, I will continue to pour in.

For this is a nation, a world who requires the pour from My people. Don't sit in judgement of what sits or what stands before you. Don't sit in judgement based upon what you know about the individual. Don't sit in judgement. Pour as I have instructed you to do. Pour as I have given you instructions. Pour as Holy Spirit guides you. Pour into the young, the old. Pour into the babies. Pour into the seniors. Pour into the rich. Pour into the poor.

For I have opened doors for you saith the Lord God Almighty. Doors and places. I have given you a seat at the table, pour. Do not question, Why am I here? I have called you to this place. And as you come to this place in obedience, the pour must happen. Pour saith God. Tune your ears in closer so you can hear what to pour. Lay out before me. Stretch out before me like you use to in your quiet place. Stretch out in your secret place and wait to hear what I have to say to you. For many of you, you will see it. You will begin to see faces. You will begin to hear names. And as I give that to you, I will place you in the same space where they are. And you will know because Holy Spirit will allow you to recognize the face, the name I have given you. And as you open your mouth, do not question What am I to say? For I have filled your mouth.

Speak saith God. Pour into them. I remind you again, do not sit in judgement based upon what you know. These are My children.

These are the ones I have called from the other fold. These are the ones I have sent you to. Do not sit in judgement. Pour saith God. I have equipped you. I have positioned you. I have shifted you to a new level, to another place.

Guard the anointing that is in you. Guard the anointing that is upon you because I need you in this hour to pour. Mind what you hear. Mind what you listen to. Mind what you allow in your spirit. Mind those from your past who are coming into your now, not for your good but for destruction. Open your eyes and see saith God. Do not fear. I have not given you the spirit of fear, but I have given you love, power and a sound mind. You will know them. You will see them. You will feel the uneasiness in your spirit. You will see them. You will see their heart and you will know how to stand up against. You will know what weapon to deploy. For that matter stay fully equipped, fully dressed, fully endowed with power from on high, fully knowledgeable of My word.

POUR SAITH THE LORD

Beautiful But Broken

"To appoint unto them that mourn in Zion, to give unto them beauty for ashes, the oil of joy for mourning, the garment of praise for the spirit of heaviness; that they might be called trees of righteousness, the planting of the LORD, that he might be glorified." -Isaiah 61:3 KJV

Sometimes we sit with the pain of broken pieces in a beautiful place. Shattered but held in place. Simply because of what God's hands has made us of. Yet, we stand in need of repairing. The old need to be removed and replaced with the new. This requires a skilled individual. A master, skilled in his craft who can remove the broken pieces without damaging or destroying the shell.

Often we pour from a cracked vessel. It's leaky, messy and unable to fully accomplish what's needed. It can't sustain us either. The more we pour, the more we leak. The more we leak, the weaker we get. Simply because we push past the pain, tiredness and weakness refusing to stop, regroup, replenish and heal.

The Father is saying: Let the Master hands of Jesus repair the crack(s) before you have a major break. Let Him remove the old and make you new. He won't damage or destroy. He'll preserve and beautify you. He'll exchange the ashes for beauty, the mourning for the oil of joy, the spirit of heaviness for a garment of praise. Steal away and take care of you. Rest, restoration, and relaxation is the order of the day.

Just Because of Christ

April

Hannah Jones

Meet Hannah Jones

Hannah Jones is a mezzo-soprano from Houston, Texas in her first year in The Metropolitan Opera's Lindemann Young Artist Development Program, where she joined the Met's 2024 Summer Parks Recital Series as part of the City Parks Foundation's SummerStage Festival.

During the 2024–25 season, she made her Met debut as one of the voices of the Unborn Children in Die Frau ohne Schatten and made her company debut as Jennie Jackson in the world premiere of Tazewell Thompson's Jubilee at Seattle Opera.

Later this season, she will cover the role of Iras in the Met's premiere of John Adams's Antony and Cleopatra. Previous operatic engagements include covering Monisha in Joplin's Treemonisha and Mrs. McLean in Floyd's Susannah with Opera Theater of Saint Louis, Hermia in Britten's A Midsummer Night's Dream, and Maman/La Libellule in Ravel's L'Enfant et les sortilèges at the Manhattan School of Music.

She has performed on ABC's Good Morning America with The Denyce Graves Foundations' Shared Voices program, and in concert performances with Opera for Peace in Rome, Italy.

In 2024, she was named Winner of the DC-Maryland-Virginia District and recipient of the Encouragement Award from the Eastern Region of the Met's Laffont Competition. Later that year, she won second place in the Manhattan School of Music's Alan M. and Joan Taub Ades Vocal Competition and received the Richard F. Gold Career Grant from the Shoshana Foundation.

She is an alumna of the Gerdine Young Artist Program at Opera Theatre of Saint Louis, the Seagle Festival Emerging Artist Program, and was a member of the inaugural cohort of The Denyce Graves Foundations' Shared Voices program. She holds degrees in voice from Lawrence University and the Manhattan School of Music.

As Hannah's light shines bright in the opera industry, she credits Jesus Christ as her source and reason for success.

What's On Your Private Story?

When I was in undergrad, I was at the pinnacle of living a double life. We don't need to go into details of that today Just know your girl was wildin' out. I wasn't afraid of what people thought of me, but I was afraid of my parents finding out. To be honest, I was inherently more afraid of disappointing my parents than disappointing God. This wasn't because it was instilled in me by someone. The enemy knew how much I love and respected my parents and would use that to keep me in shame and bondage. Maybe I'll share my testimony of how I got delivered from that bondage next week (Buckle up).

One of the things I would utilize heavily during that time of my life was the private story feature on Instagram. Now, don't get me wrong. I love private stories because sometimes you don't want everybody to know your business. Main story: Nice cute image Private story: _____.

Now, I don't know why Hannah did all of that extra work when God, the Omniscient One, could see ALL of that. When we're deep in sin, it's truly amazing how we will construct some kind of false ideology to justify our behavior.

"I'll just ask for forgiveness later.."

"I'm sorry, God, but I need this."

"God knows my heart"

The fact is, God does in fact knows our hearts, and 9 times of 10 our hearts are filthy. Let's take a look at what Jesus says about this:

Matthew 15:17-19

17 "Anything you eat passes through the stomach and then goes into the sewer. 18 But the words you speak come from the heart—that's what defiles you. 19 For from the heart come evil thoughts, murder, adultery, all sexual immorality, theft, lying, and slander. (NLT)

The truth of the matter is that WE DON'T HAVE TIME TO LIVE DOUBLE LIVES. If you proclaim to be a follower of Jesus Christ, yet you don't follow any of His instructions, THIS IS THE TIME TO REPENT and turn away from your sinful behavior and habits. When I was OUT there, I, number 1, did not truly fear God, and number 2, I thought I had time. "I'll tighten up when I get older". Yall, God is calling us to live in holiness NOW (1 Thessalonians 4:7).

No one, not even the angels in heaven know when God will return for His people, and because of that we must get ready and stay ready. God loves us so much that He sent his only and perfect son, Jesus Christ, to die for our sins (John 3:16). If you're reading this, PRAISE GOD because He has given you the opportunity to dedicate your life to Him.

You are not a lost cause, and you are not too far gone. It doesn't matter how many times you've broken promises to God. Anything telling you that God hates you is A LIE FROM THE PITS OF HELL. GOD LOVES YOU SO MUCH. Give your life to Him today. Do away with the double life, and live for Jesus!

What next:
Ask the Holy Spirit to reveal the things that you need to repent of. If you have any habits, addictions, etc., ask the LORD to reveal the root of these things. May His Holy Spirit deal with these things for you, and may you be delivered from them in Jesus Name!

Throw away any idols or things of your old nature. Literally, throw them away
Start reading your Bible DAILY(Proverbs 7:1-3)

Start praying DAILY

Romans 6:23

For the wages of sin is death, but the [a]gift of God is eternal life in Christ Jesus our Lord.

Asking For Forgiveness

I can attest that it was always easier for me to remember and hold on to the bad things someone has done or said to me. My response would often result in cutting them off. No conversation of nothing. You're getting blocked.

On the flip side, it wasn't as easy for me to remember the hurtful things I've done or said to others. Further down the line, the Holy Spirit would convict me of these things, but out of pride and shame, I didn't want to face that reality…..so what would I do to avoid the truth? I'd cut that person out of my life. Blocked. I know…that's just ridiculous and ungodly.

Matthew 5:23-24
23 Therefore, if you are bringing an offering to God and you remember that your brother is angry at you or holds a grudge against you, 24 then leave your gift before the altar, go to your brother, repent and forgive one another, be reconciled, and then return to the altar to offer your gift to God.

Jesus tells us to go deal with the problem head on! Admit your wrongdoings, don't do it again, and ask for forgiveness from our brothers and sisters. This was a very difficult task for me in the beginning. I always had to be right. It was always my way or get blocked, but all of that was pride. We are not always right. Our feelings matter, but they should not be the only ones that matter.

I encourage you not to run away. Ask the Holy Spirit to reveal to you those you might've offended and hurt. Even if it has been years, apologize with a sincere heart and ask them for forgiveness TODAY. If the situation is big or small or even if you don't think you were in the wrong, ask the LORD to help you understand and to guide your words.

Note: They may or may not forgive you right away, but the important part is that you humble yourself before God and your brothers and sisters.

Blessings!

May

Wendy Dangerfield- Jones

Meet Wendy Dangerfield Jones

I'm simply a lover of God and His people—not a theologian, just someone captivated by the richness and depth of His Word. My life has been shaped by His extraordinary hand, and everything I am flows from that place.

Over the years, God has allowed me to serve in many capacities—Children's Church Director, praise and worship leader, prayer team leader, administrative assistant, small group Bible study leader, and outreach minister. Today, I serve alongside my husband, Pastor Steve Jones, through Pneuma Global Ministries and Pleasant Hill Church of Deliverance under the leadership of Pastor Gene and Lady Gail Johnson. Whether within the church walls or beyond them, my heart is to reach people where they are—with love, truth, and hope.

At my core, I'm a seer, a storyteller, and, most importantly, a witness to the extraordinary love of Jesus Christ—a love I know deeply. It's that love that compels me to spend my days pouring it back into others.

I'm someone who simply loves people—serving, encouraging, and helping however I can. One of my deepest passions is nurturing young women through Bible study, fellowship, and real-world support, believing that God's extraordinary love meets us in even the most ordinary places.

I was honored to study under Dr. Cindy Trimm at the Kingdom School of Ministry and under the late Bishop William McKnight of Calvary Worship Center, Baytown. Still, my greatest lessons have come through walking closely with the Lord—through the joys, battles, and everyday miracles that mark a life surrendered to Him.

Professionally, I'm a Project Management Professional (PMP), consultant, and investor. I've been blessed to build a dynamic career at the intersection of marketing, technology, strategy, and purpose, as co-founder of Mighty Strategic Consulting, leader of The Transformula, and co-owner of Pneuma Global Logistics with my husband. Real estate has also become a space where God continues to open doors for stewardship.

In 2021, I was honored to be selected as one of only a few from tens of thousands of applicants for Tulsa Remote—a prestigious program that brings professionals to live and work in Tulsa, Oklahoma. That experience opened new doors both personally and professionally, including opportunities on and off Greenwood, also known as Black Wall Street. I also volunteered with Reading Partners, helping students in underserved schools build strong foundations in reading and confidence.

Community service has always been integral to my life. I recently reactivated my membership with Top Ladies of Distinction, Inc. (TLOD), a national nonprofit dedicated to enhancing the lives of youth and adults through programs focused on education, leadership development, and community service. Through TLOD's youth affiliate, Top Teens of America (TTA), I will continue to mentor and support initiatives that empower our young people.

I'm a proud University of Houston alum, holding a Bachelor of Arts in RTV. As I continue making my mark in the tech space, I'm preparing to pursue advanced studies in Artificial Intelligence—trusting God to enlarge every territory He's called me to influence.

When Dr. Wiley and I reconnected at The Woods last year with Lady Gail, I told her, "I'm ready!" Buuuut what I meant was: I'm ready to give, support from behind the scenes, quietly serve—my comfort zone these days. I've had my fill of the spotlight, if you will. But over the past year, while walking through one of the most stretching, sacred, and faith-deepening seasons of my life, God has continued to nudge me forward. And honestly, I know that holding back would be less about humility and more about hesitation and disobedience. So this time, my "yes" isn't about position or being seen, it's about obedience. Wherever He leads, I'll follow.

Each devotional you read in May flows from that "yes," plus real faith, real reflection. A reminder that no matter where you are, Abba Father is already there, weaving every thread together for His glory.

Arise & Move

It's wild to realize we're already in May—the fifth month of the year, biblically connected to the number of grace. But today isn't just another date on the calendar. It's Day 13 of the Omer—the stretch of time on God's calendar between Passover and Pentecost, between coming out of Egypt and receiving the fire of Sinai.

This space—the in-between—is sacred.

As I sat with that, a few words or descriptors kept stirring: Transition. Movement. Shifting. Letting go of what was and walking toward what's next.

But if we're honest, this is also the part of the year where momentum starts to fade.
We begin to wonder if we heard God right back in December or January, crossing over into the new year.
The pace picks up. The weight gets heavier.
What felt clear at the start now feels buried under responsibilities, disappointment, and delay.

It's not that we've given up—it's that we're tired in the middle.

And I think that's where many of us are.

Not where we were, but not yet where we know we're going.
Freed, but still being formed.
Called, but not yet fully walking in the thing.

That's exactly where the children of Israel were—delivered but still developing.
God brought them out, but they hadn't yet stepped into the full promise.
And that space between—the desert, the stretch, the not yet—was where their character, their trust, and their obedience were shaped.

I believe the same is true for us now.

You've come through a lot.
You've laid things down. You've crossed over.
But now you're in the tension.
You feel the pull to keep going—but everything in your flesh wants to pause.

Here's the word:
Don't stop moving!

* This is not the time to shrink back.
* This is not the time to settle into survival mode or comfort zones.
* And it's definitely not the time to wait for conditions to be perfect.

God is still speaking.
And a generation is still waiting to hear the sound you carry.
This moment matters—not just for you, but for the people assigned to your voice, your life, your obedience.

Isaiah 30:21 says,
"You will hear a voice behind you saying, 'This is the way. Walk in it.'"

Even if you've drifted, even if you've delayed—He's still speaking.
He's still directing. And He's still expecting movement.
Don't let weariness lie to you.

Don't let what's happening in the systems of this world distract you from the assignment of the Kingdom.
Don't let the absence of support convince you that the vision no longer matters.
It still matters. You still matter.

- So speak life over what you buried.
- Pick up what you dropped and walk in boldness and grace.

You truly don't need another confirmation—you need the reminder, the courage to act on the one you already received.

This is Kingdom ground.
And Kingdom ground doesn't wait for approval to be taken.

So today, this is your declaration:
"I will not wait for perfect conditions—I move in divine timing.
I will not fear the future—God is already there.
I will not retreat—I was born for this.
I arise. I move. I obey."

"Arise, for your light has come!
And the glory of the Lord is rising on you!

May the fresh wind of God—the ruach—blow on you now.
May His fresh oil pour over and saturate you now.
You need it to keep moving.
"Not by might, nor by power, but by My Spirit," says the Lord." -Zechariah 4:6

The Power of a Servant

"She said to her mistress, 'If only my master would see the prophet who is in Samaria! He would cure him of his leprosy."
-2 Kings 5:3 (NIV)

She was nameless, yet not powerless.
She had no title. No pulpit. No platform.
She was a servant girl in a pagan household—not by choice, but by force.
And yet… she spoke.

A young Hebrew girl, taken captive and reduced to servitude, became the unlikely vessel used to bring healing to a man and honor to her God. She wasn't named a prophet, warrior, or ruler—a girl in the background, "just" a SERVANT. But when she spoke to her mistress, everything began to change.

There is a prophet in Samaria. There is a God who heals.

Because she spoke up, a man was healed, and a pagan nation witnessed the power of Israel's God.

Naaman was a decorated military commander—mighty in rank, favor, and battle. But he had leprosy. And for all his greatness, he hadn't experienced healing.

Until a servant girl pointed the way.

Her simple words set in motion a chain of events that led Naaman to the prophet Elisha, and Naaman was healed. And through his healing, a pagan nation witnessed the undeniable power of Israel's God.

This handmaiden could have remained silent. She had every reason to be bitter, broken, and bound by the weight of her situation. (So, let Naaman live with this disease… oh well)

But she didn't choose silence. While the Scripture makes no mention of her feelings or character, her action speaks for her. She didn't have a platform, but she had a word.

She didn't have position, but she carried power.

To the One Who Feels Unseen & Overlooked….You may feel hidden. Small. Assigned to a space you didn't choose.
But your voice still matters. It holds the key for someone God has called you to reach.
This isn't to minimize the role of the pulpit or the formal ministry positions—those are vital.

But don't miss this:
God doesn't need a spotlight, a platform, or a viral moment. He just needs a willing you— someone who isn't chasing visibility, but ready to be used right where you are.
Someone who will simply open their mouth.

Hear this:
Like the handmaiden:

- You don't need a man-given title to be a vessel.
- You don't need recognition to carry revelation.
- You don't need status to shift a season.

God's power isn't restricted by any of that.

This is your moment to speak. Tell somebody what you know about your God!
- Speak life in the workplace where darkness has taken root.
- Speak hope to the man drowning in despair.
- Speak truth in a culture addicted to lies.
- Speak healing over the wounded and bound.

Simply point them to the One who is able to save, heal, deliver, and set free!

Yes, you may feel nameless on earth, but your name is surely known in heaven.
The impact of your words will outlive you, and what you release in faith will echo through generations.

And listen!
You are not too old—your work is not done.
You are not too young—your voice Is absolutely necessary.

God is using the willing, not just the known.

You may not realize what's being set in motion when you open your mouth—but Heaven does.

So speak. Testify. Obey. And let God do what only He can through you.

What if the next major move of God is waiting… on you, servant?

June

Helen Miller

Meet Helen Miller

My life journey is truly a testimony of God's unrelenting grace and presence. I was born with childhood asthma, praise God I am healed from it. However, looking back, I realize the enemy tried to take my life at a young age, because I was constantly hospitalized due to severe asthma attacks. I was raised by my mother in a single-parent home with my brother. Though life wasn't always easy, God made sure we were never without the essentials.

I am proud to be a wife, and a mother of four. Interestingly, each of our children are born five years apart. My brother and I share the same five year age gap. That wasn't intentional but I like to say it is confirmation of our family's grace. Grace follows, covers and leads us.

Everything I am and have become is anchored in the unwavering foundation laid early in my life by my relationship with God and the church. Church wasn't just something we attended, it was part of our lifestyle. I received Christ as my Lord and Savior while at home, in my room. I am grateful for the foundation, because it was the leaning post I knew to come back when I tried to stray One of my greatest educational honors, was being the first person in my immediate family to graduate from college, and the first on my mother's side to earn a graduate degree.

Philippians 4:12 is my life testimony, "I know what it is to be in need, and I know what it is to have plenty. I have learned the secret of being content in any and every situation."

In every season of life, I've found new strength, new joy, and new reasons to lean on my lifeline scripture, Proverbs 3:5-6, Trust in the Lord with all your heart and lean not on your own understanding; in all your ways submit to Him, and He will make your paths straight.

I love my church, Chosen Church of Houston and my husband happens to be the pastor. It's more than a church for me, it's a community that pushes me closer to God, deeper into purpose, and forward in faith. Through my community of faith, I continue to grow as a woman of God, wife, mother, and leader.

Outside of ministry and motherhood, I find joy in traveling, especially to Caribbean destinations. The peace of the islands remind me of God's rest, refreshment, and beauty. My story is evolving and I am grateful to be in covenant with Our Heavenly Father through My Lord and Savior Jesus.

God Is NOT Distant!

He's very much Omnipresent and attentive to your cry. You DON'T have to whisper your pain or hide your tears. When life feels overwhelming and silent, be reminded that your voice echoes in Heaven. He is the Deliverer who listens, responds, and rescues in His perfect time.

Today, take comfort in knowing that your prayers are heard and help is on the way. Pick your head UP, stick your chest out, KNOWING FULL WELL, He hears you!

TESTIMONY: My father was not consistently present in my brother's and my life after my parents got divorced. Fast forward to my sophomore year at Texas Southern University, I was what they called 'a poor, struggling college student.' Rent was due, and I had never been late, so I went to the leasing office to petition for a grace period. It was stated in the lease, and when I applied, they made it clear that no rent would be accepted beyond the 5th, and no partial payments would be accepted. It was the 3rd, and I had no actual plan on how to get the remaining balance. I was short due to being laid off.

The leasing agent asked the apartment manager if they could make an exception for me, as I was a college student, a good tenant, and had never been late with my rent. Shocking, both came to a mutual agreement. I left the office grateful for the extension until the 15th, but in my mind, I'm thinking, 'Lord, where is the money coming from?' Unemployment was pending. I go to my apartment, pray, and put my phone on silent. I told myself, 'Don't stress or cry because it's not going to change anything.' I went to sleep and woke up to multiple missed calls from my favorite cousin. She left several voicemails, saying, "Girl, answer your phone!" I called her; she was reaching out to tell me that my dad, whom I hadn't heard from in years, caught the bus to my childhood church and left an envelope full of money with my uncle (the pastor) for my brother and me. As I flew out the door to my car, my mind was still trying to process because it made NO SENSE, in nature, for things to play out like that and that fast. It was a substantial amount of money; I paid my rent for three months and paid off my car note and insurance for a few months. My dad and I reconnected after I had longed to see him for years. That was one of the moments when I realized that God had honestly answered, and here's my prayer.

"The righteous cry out, and the Lord hears them; he delivers them from all their troubles." -Psalm 34:17

Stronghold Breaker

Strongholds may have lasted years, which can feel like an eternity in terms of their impact on your mental, emotional, and spiritual health. However, I want all of my family in Christ to know and affirm that your breaking point is not your final destination! It's just a point in your journey. God's Word promises freedom from anything that tries to bind you. Shame, fear, or failure MUST bow to the authority of Jesus. Stand tall, head up, chest out again, knowing full well that deliverance & freedom are YOUR portion.

Now, I will break their yoke from your neck and tear your shackles away. Nahum 1:13

ACTION PLAN

1. Acknowledge the Stronghold (from a place of awareness, not agreement)

Ask the Holy Spirit to reveal root causes: patterns, pain, trauma, or agreements that gave the stronghold access (John 8:32). Write out behaviors, thoughts, or cycles you're struggling with. Be specific, transparent, and honest. This will activate transformation (deliverance) over time.

Declare: This stops with me! I am not what I went through. HOWEVER, I am who God says I am!

2. Renounce & Repent (Break Agreement)

Renounce - To officially reject, disown, or break agreement with sin, lies, or anything opposed to God's will.

Repent- To turn away from sin with godly sorrow and turn toward God with a changed heart and mindset.

Renounce any sin(s) connected to the stronghold (fear, shame, pride, addiction, etc.). Repent and declare freedom in Christ. This may seem like a dramatic step, but you can write a "Break-Up Letter" to declare what you're walking away from and why you chose God's freedom.

Declare: I no longer partner with fear, shame, or bondage. I walk in liberty through Christ. Check out this song to add more season to this action step: Fear Is Not My Future (feat. Tasha Cobbs Leonard) & Todd Galberth

3. Replace It With Truth

Seek out scriptures that oppose the stronghold and declare them daily! Post the scriptures where you can see them often.

Declare: My mind is renewed!

4. Renew & Rewire Daily

Begin each day with prayer and worship. Be intentional about practicing habits that support healing.

5. Walk It Out in the Community

Get connected to the Kingdom of God Community (local church, a prayer group, etc. A Kingdom Tribe that provides accountability, encouragement, AND celebrates your progress.

July

Prudence Oppong

Meet Prudence Oppong

Prudence Oppong, a Family Nurse Practitioner, balances her professional and personal life. She's married and lives in Sugarland, TX.

Prudence finds joy in singing and dancing. She actively contributes to her local church choir. Her aspirations include mentoring and leading others, with a focus on the bereaved and young individuals.

Her ministry centers around praise and worship, counseling, intercession, and guiding others to Christ.

When to Retreat For Battle

"And when the Pharisees went forth and straightway took counsel with Herodians against him, how they might destroy him. But Jesus withdrew himself with his disciples to the sea and a great multitude from Galilee followed him and from Judaea." - Mark 3:6-7 (KJV)

When the Pharisees sought to kill Jesus after He healed the sick on the Sabbath, He withdrew and relocated Himself and His disciples to a different territory—the sea. There, the Pharisees were unable to reach him. Perhaps the Pharisees lacked boats or were simply unable to swim. As you can imagine, fighting on the water or in a boat just sounds simply logistically challenging!

Sometimes we have to remove ourselves from the enemy's territory (ground) and retreat to the "sea" —a safe zone, a different territory that is not accessible to the enemy. We must consider retreating to a different location, just as Jesus went with His disciples.

Sometimes we may need to not only remove ourselves from the current situation but seek the company of Godly people to fortify oneself.

Prayer: Father teach me when to engage in combat and when to simply retreat to a safe zone. In Jesus Name. Amen!

Power and Dominion

"Every place that the sole of your foot shall tread upon, that have I given unto you, as I said unto Moses. (V.5) There shall not any man be able to stand before thee all the days of thy life; as I was with Moses, so I will be with the: I will not fail thee, nor forsake the." - Joshua 1:3, 5 (KJV)

This verse is such a profound assurance that we have been given the power and dominion over any situation to cause it to shift to our benefit wherever we are. I wonder how often we exercise that authority in our lives, our families, or work places.

Do you realize what it means to have dominion over wherever your feet touches?

That means that when we step anywhere we can take charge by simply commanding by faith, every power or situation to be subdued under the power of the Holy Spirit within us. Yes, we can cause the atmosphere to shift in accordance with the will of God. All we have to do is declare it and it is so! And that's not all, the bible says that no one can stand before us, he will be with us like he was with Moses and he will not fail nor forsake us (VS. 5). What a privilege!

PRAYER: Father I thank you for clothing me with the righteousness of Jesus Christ and granting me the power of your holy spirit to take charge wherever my feet steps. I thank you that you are with me and will never leave nor forsake me. In Jesus Name!

August

Michelle Cardwell

Meet Michelle Cardwell

Michelle Cardwell was born and raised in New York City. She is the devoted wife of Eric Cardwell and proud mother to Chelsea Nicholson, Christian Cardwell, and son-in-love Tremell Nicholson. Her greatest joy comes from being "Gigi" to her cherished grandchildren: Layla, Jayden, Tremell, and Kirra.

Michelle has dedicated her life to serving others through prayer, worship, and encouragement. She is a Certified Christian Counselor, Chaplain, and a certified member of the Women of Valour Emergency Response Team under Dr. Allison Wiley. Her passion for worship and intercession shines through her involvement in many church ministries.

She was ordained Prophetess and Apostle under the leadership of Bishop Glen Jeffery and Apostle Shanita Jeffery. Michelle has contributed her writings to the book Heart Check (compiled by Apostle Shanita Jeffery), Revivalist (compiled by Dr. Allison

Wiley & WOV Inspirational Leaders), and recently From Bondage to Freedom (compiled by Vinoka Moses).

Michelle currently serves a leader with the Women of Significance Ministry, where she works alongside Pastor Gwendolyn Graham and Elder Ida Benjamin to empower, equip and uplift women.

In her spare time, Michelle enjoys reading, knitting, crocheting, and spending quality time with her family. Her daily affirmation remains a guiding light: "I know with God all things are possible."

The Time Is Now

There are moments in life when God stirs our spirit with an urgency that cannot be ignored. Often, we wait thinking tomorrow will be better, easier, or clearer. But Scripture repeatedly points us back to the present moment. God calls us to move now not in fear or haste, but in obedience and trust.

You Were Made for This Moment & Time

"And who knows but that you have come to your royal position for such a time as this?"
— Esther 4:14 (NIV)

Esther's story is about divine timing. She didn't seek out her position as queen it was orchestrated by God. When her people were in danger, her cousin Mordecai challenged her with this truth: Maybe this is exactly why you're here.

Many of us underestimate the purpose behind our current season. You may think you're in a job, relationship, or role by coincidence, but God's hand is in it. Don't overlook where He has positioned you. He may be calling you to speak up, lead, or take a bold step that affects others beyond yourself.

Reflection:
Where has God placed you "for such a time as this"? Wherever it is respond in obedience rather than fear.

Stay Rooted in Truth

Theme Scripture: Matthew 24:4 (NIV)
"Jesus answered: Watch out that no one deceives you."

Deception isn't always obvious. In fact, that's what makes it so dangerous, especially when it comes from within the church. It often comes cloaked in charisma, clever speech, and partial truths. It can sound spiritual, use the name of Jesus, and even quote scripture—but be completely off from God's intent. That's why spiritual discernment is so vital. Jesus Himself warned that in the last days, "many will come in My name, claiming, 'I am the Messiah,' and will deceive many" (Matthew 24:5). He also said that false messengers would perform great signs and wonders, aiming to mislead, "if possible, even the elect" (Matthew 24:24, NIV). The sobering reality is that not all who stand behind a pulpit are preaching truth, and not every popular voice in Christian culture is being led by the Holy Spirit.

False teachings are rarely blatant. They often sound good, feel good, and even carry a hint of truth—just enough to seem biblical. But anything that twists God's Word or leads people away from repentance, holiness, and Christ-centered living is not from God. Messages that promote self over surrender, pleasure over purity, or blessings without obedience are dangerous distortions of the gospel.

2 Timothy 4:3–4 (NIV) warns us clearly: "For the time will come when people will not put up with sound doctrine. Instead, to suit their own desires, they will gather around them a great number of teachers to say what their itching ears want to hear." We're living in that time now. Many seek spiritual affirmation rather than biblical transformation. They want motivational speeches instead of sanctifying truth. People are drawn to leaders who affirm their lifestyles rather than challenge them to live in alignment with God's Word. As a result, entire congregations are being built on emotional hype, worldly values, or watered-down theology.

The Apostle Paul also cautioned the church that Satan masquerades as an angel of light (2 Corinthians 11:14), and his servants do the same. That's why it's not enough to simply be impressed by someone's gift; we must test their fruit and doctrine. Emotionalism is not the same as anointing. Popularity is not a sign of spiritual authority. We must be rooted in the Word and guided by the Holy Spirit, not swayed by personality or performance. It's critical for all of us as believers to become students of the Word examining every message, every spirit, and every teaching through the lens of Scripture, just as the Bereans did in Acts 17:11. Our foundation must be truth, not trends.

Reflection:
Have I grown comfortable with spiritual messages that make me feel good but don't challenge me to grow?

September

Alysa Elliott- Wilson

Meet Alysa Elliott-Wilson

Alysa Elliott-Wilson is a dedicated leader, advocate and servant whose life's work has been rooted in service to families, children and her faith community.

Originally from Orange, Texas Alysa called Houston home for the past 20 years. She holds a Bachelor of Science degree in Management and Marketing from McNeese state University that has supported her work in both the public and Faith-Based sectors.

With over 35 years of experience in the child welfare system, Alysa currently serves as the Regional Administrator for Faith-Based and Community Engagement at the Texas Department of Family and Protective Services. In this role, she and her Team work tirelessly to build partnerships that support and strengthen vulnerable children and families in the Houston and Outlying county areas.

She is the founder of REGAL Ministries, which stands for Restoration,

Encouragement, Grace And Love – the core elements and foundational principles by which she lives and serves. Through this ministry, she seeks to uplift and restore those in need, always guided by compassion and purpose.

Beyond her professional work and personal ambition, Alysa is a licensed Minister at House of Glory Houston serving under the Leadership of Teacher Tommy Jones and Apostle Kimberly Jackson-Jones. Alysa leads the Altar Ministry Team, offering support and guidance to those seeking healing and connection with God.

She became a certified Leadership Facilitator for the In Search of Purpose…En route to Destiny – a 14-week appointment with God Curriculum in January 2017. Alysa continues to serve as a Facilitator for various inner healing curriculums, helping others find clarity through Faith-Based teaching and counseling.

Alysa is the proud daughter of the late Reverand Shirley Allen-Jenkins, whose legacy of Faith, strength and service continues to inspire her. She lives each day committed to carrying that legacy forward by being a Christian example in both word and action.

Above all, Alysa is a devoted mother of three adult children – Bryson, Cameron and Kennedy – who are a continual source of pride and joy.

Alysa's life is a testament to purpose, perseverance and power of a surrendered life to Jesus Christ.

Our God Reigns!

Accepting God's Kingship means acknowledging Him as the Ultimate Authority in our life. It also means allowing Him to guide our decisions and surrendering our desire for control. There is much going on in our world today. So many debates, so many "authorities and authority figures" spouting rhetoric, informing us of what is "right" and how things should be. I've seen a lot of it on social media lately… and I'm sure you have as well either on social media or in the news.

We can all get caught up in our feelings and emotions in listening to debates and discord about societal issues. However, I want to remind each of you today that no matter what political, religious, spiritual or social concern that is attempting to lead you to believe one way or another that the Final Authority is Jesus Christ!!!

We must rely on The Word of God which never changes to guide us. The Word is not a matter of opinion, but biblical facts. Our faith and obedience need to be found in it and not controlled by earthly emotions. God's grace will empower us to live righteously and overcome challenges. In doing this, we can live a life led by peace, purpose, and spiritual victory.

God is the supreme King! He holds authority over all earthly authority, creation and every aspect of our lives. "For through Him God created everything in the heavenly realms and on earth. He made the things we can see and the things we can't see - such as thrones, kingdoms, rulers, and authorities in the unseen world. Everything was created through Him and for Him. Colossians 1:16

God is not distant but actively involved, orchestrating events that we see around us. As Christians and believers, we can actively pray for God's Will to be done. No matter how things may seem or appear around us, we must remember that God – who is The Authority has a way of working everything out for our good and His purpose.

Friend, I encourage you today to accept Jesus' Reign in your life as well as reigning in our neighborhood, community, city, state, nation and the world. We must actively live above the circumstances we see on social media and the news, overcome the temptation to judge and condemn others. We should not be ruled by our flesh, but instead, walk in divine wisdom and power! In doing this we will not be controlled by the inclinations to address the problems and issues around us as we see fit. As a community and nation of people, we are all affected by decisions made by those with authority in the "earth realm". However, as Kingdom citizens, we have the Authority to take every concern to God in prayer!!!

Use Your Authority to make your requests known to God. He Reigns Supreme and has the Ultimate Authority and final say.

Do You Think Your Life Is Your Own?

Today, I will be brief… but want to share a dream I had circa 15 years ago.

I was standing in the mirror looking at myself. All of a sudden, I noticed (and had never noticed this before) a long, dusty-rose colored rope hanging out the clavicle bone in my neck! I was an adult woman in my dream. Which meant this rope had been on my all of my life. I begin to tug and pull on it in an attempt to remove it. I tugged aggressively to extract it out of my neck, however, it was IMMOVABLE! That rope had no leeway and did not move!

Innately (again... in my dream) I had the clear and distinct "knowing" that my mother knew that rope was hanging off my clavicle bone. And she was aware that I was born with it! I begin to ponder why she never had the rope removed. Afterall, how could she have let me go all my life with a rope hanging down my body!!!

As the dream continued, I began to walk out of the bathroom to go and discuss this with her. Well, let me be honest… I was going to go and "confront" my Mother for having me walk around for years with that old dusty-rose rope hanging down my body! As I took one step out of the bathroom to look for my mother, I heard an audible Voice say "STOP"!!! I stood frozen… The Voice continued… that rope is from Me!!! It was at that point in my dream, I looked down… and at the bottom of the rope was a white price tag. The Voice continued… That rope is covered with My blood… I paid a price for YOU!!!

I immediately began weeping in my dream. I woke up and fell on my knees on the side of my bed. I begin to cry uncontrollably. When I was able to get myself together, I prayed and asked the Lord to forgive me. I knew it was to Him that I owed my life!!! He was my redeemer. I then pulled a tablet out of my nightstand and began to write a love letter to the Lord. I apologized profusely for thinking that my life was my own and that I could do what I wanted with "my life and my body". It was then, that I made a promise… a vow to God!!! I told Him, whatever He wanted me to say… I would say it. And whatever, He wanted me to do… I would do it!

Since that day, crying and weeping on the side of my bed, I have tried to keep my promise to my Heavenly Father. I realized then and now more than ever… I AM NOT MY OWN!!! My walk with Christ, is not perfect. However, I trust The Lord will perfect that which concerns me! His mercies endure forever! I will not forsake the work of His hands. I thank God He continues to perfect the things He desires in me. { Psalm 138:8} I am obedient and submitted.

Friends, we are bought with a price.

Therefore, we must glorify God in our bodies. When God paid the price of His Son to purchase us from sin, guilt and condemnation it was the ransom for our body and soul. {1 Corinthians 6:20}

This is not a lay-a-way plan!!! He paid the price for us IN FULL!!! That payment was a complete sacrifice, meaning there is no balance left to be paid and no further debt to us. We must remember, the Price He paid for us was costly!!! That price was not cheap or of human value! Instead, it was a severe and extravagant sacrifice – that left our Precious Father battered, bruised, bloodied and marred before His death and ultimate resurrection! God did this for us... out of His GREAT LOVE!!!

Through that dream, Jesus not only showed me that I belonged to Him. He also reminded me that I was bought with a cost. If you are reading this... do KNOW... You were bought with a cost too!!! As a matter of fact, at the same time as when He died for me!!! Glory!!!

JESUS PAID THE FULL PRICE, ONCE AND FOR ALL!!!

Heavenly Father, we come before You with hearts full of gratitude. Thank you for paying the ultimate price for sending Your Son, Jesus Christ to die on the cross for our sins. You gave up everything so that we might be forgiven, redeemed and brought into right relationship with You. Lord, forgive us for the times we've lived for ourselves. For the moments we've chased our own desires and forgotten Your grace.

We repent of our self-centered ways and surrender our lives back to You. Thank You for Your mercy that never fails and for Your love that never gives up on us. Help us to walk in a way that honors You. May our thoughts, our words, and our actions bring You glory. Teach us to live not for ourselves, but for YOU – the One who gave everything for us. In all that we do, may we seek what pleases You. Shape our hearts to reflect Your will and lead us in paths of righteousness for Your name's sake.

We pray this in the POWERFUL and Holy Name of Jesus. Amen.

October

Ashley Baxter

Meet Ashley Baxter

First and foremost, Ashley Baxter is a daughter of the King and a devoted follower of Jesus. Everything she does flows out of her love for Him and her desire to see His Kingdom advance on earth. She is also a wife to Kevin Baxter and the proud mother of two amazing young ladies, believing her home is her first and most important ministry.

Ashley is a licensed and ordained minister, a visionary leader, and the Founder of Mission Forward Consulting, Mission Forward Academy, and The Mission Forward Network—a Kingdom-minded movement dedicated to raising up leaders, equipping the next generation, and advancing God's purposes through Kingdom collaboration and community in every segment of society. She is passionate about the advancement and multiplication of the global Church and is a highly sought-after speaker known for her ability to connect vision to action, stir faith, and inspire impact.

Ashley served for nearly a decade as Executive Pastor at Anchor Bend Church, a thriving and life-giving church in the greater Houston area with a congregation of more than 4,000. In that role, she helped lead staff and volunteer teams of over 475 people, implementing community initiatives with both local and global reach. She directed the Anchor Bend Leadership Academy, raising up leaders who continue to serve in ministry and the marketplace, and launched The Anchor Bend Network, connecting mission-driven leaders for greater Kingdom impact. Under her leadership, the church grew in vision, generosity, and influence, including a multi-million-dollar building campaign and expanded outreach efforts that continue to bear fruit today. She now continues to serve Anchor Bend as an Associate Pastor, with a focus on teaching, preaching, and leadership development.

Alongside her ministry, Ashley brings decades of experience in the marketplace. She has held senior leadership roles in healthcare sales and business development, including Post-Acute Sales Manager for

Medtronic and Vice President of Sales for Bosch Healthcare Solutions GmbH, where she exceeded revenue targets and closed multi-million-dollar contracts. Currently, she serves as Vice President of Business Development at Connect America, where she leads and develops a national team of Sales Executives and Client Managers. She oversees a client portfolio representing more than $100 million in annual revenue and is responsible for setting the strategic vision for growth across healthcare and payor segments, including expansion into Canada. She believes strongly in marketplace ministry and carries a deep conviction that there is a revival stirring in corporate America.

Whether in the church or the marketplace, Ashley's passion is to see leaders raised up, communities transformed, and Kingdom impact multiplied. Her life's mission is to help people discover their God-given calling and move it forward with clarity, excellence, and faith.

His only begotten Son..." (John 3:16)

This is Agape love—the love that is unconditional, sacrificial, and not based on performance. The love that gives even when it's rejected. Jesus didn't come to make bad people good; He came to make dead people alive.

And when you understand His Agape love, you understand how to love yourself rightly. Jesus said:

"Love the Lord your God with all your heart,, and strength. And the second is like it: Love your neighbor as yourself."

Here's the reality: We often struggle to love others because we haven't learned how to love ourselves. If I don't see myself as forgiven, I'll struggle to forgive. If I don't believe I am worthy, I'll struggle to see worth in others. If I live in shame, I'll pass that shame onto those around me.

We have to love ourselves.

Culture defines self-love as indulgence—eating the big meal, booking the exotic vacation, buying the next thing to fill the void. But true self-love is far deeper.

Self-love means loving the real you—the person God created, the one Jesus died for. Not the image you perform for others, not the version you think you must be to earn approval, but the authentic you that is already marked by heaven.
And here's how self discipline comes in. Discipline is not restriction—it's protection. It's how you honor the real you God redeemed. Said another way, self discipline is the highest degree of self love.
When you wake up early to spend time with Jesus, you're protecting the real you.

When you forgive yourself, you're loving the real you instead of living in shame.

When you set boundaries, you're guarding the real you God created.

When you step boldly into your calling, you're saying: I agree with heaven about who I am.

Self-love is not pride—it's agreement with heaven.

Declaration Over You

I declare that you will see yourself as God sees you—worthy, chosen, and marked. I declare you will love yourself with heaven's agreement, and from that place, love others more freely. I declare that discipline will no longer feel like a burden, but like a way of protecting and honoring the real you Jesus paid for.

Lean In... To Worship

The hour is coming, and is now here, when the true worshipers will worship the Father in Spirit and in truth, for the Father is seeking such people to worship Him." (John 4:23)

God is looking. He is searching. And what He's looking for is worshipers. Not polished performances. Not empty words. But sons and daughters who lean into Him in Spirit and in truth.

Yes, worship and praise are weapons—they shift atmospheres, tear down walls, and silence the enemy. But worship is more than the songs we sing on Sunday. Worship is a lifestyle. It is how you speak. It is how you think. It is how you live.

God said in His Word: "Away with the noise of your songs! I will not listen to the music of your harps. But let justice roll on like a river, righteousness like a never-failing stream!" (Amos 5:23–24).

Why? Because true worship is not in the sound of your voice but in the posture of your heart. "The sacrifices of God are a broken spirit; a broken and contrite heart, O God, you will not despise." (Psalm 51:17).

And when we live this way, our worship rises to Him as a fragrance. "Christ loved us and gave Himself up for us as a fragrant offering and sacrifice to God." (Ephesians 5:2).

Sometimes worship is as simple as thanksgiving. Gratitude is a form of worship that disarms the enemy. "Let them offer sacrifices of thanksgiving and tell of His deeds with songs of joy." (Psalm 107:22).

So today—thank Him. Thank Him for the breath in your lungs. Thank Him for your family. Thank Him for your health. Thank Him for provision. Thank Him even for the struggle and the trial, because He is using it to shape you. Thank Him that you can hold His Word in your hands. Thank Him that here in America we still have the freedom to declare His name out loud.

Gratitude is worship. Thanksgiving is a weapon. Praise is your posture of victory.

Declaration Over You: I declare that your worship will be more than a song—it will be your life. I declare that your home will be filled with praise, your words will carry thanksgiving, and your heart will overflow with worship. I declare that as you lift up gratitude, chains will break, atmospheres will shift, and the presence of God will invade your life.

You are a true worshiper—called, chosen, and marked to worship the Father in Spirit and in truth.

Lean In...To Revival

Can you see it? Can you hear it?
Revival is sweeping across our world. There is a fresh wind of the Spirit being released: "Behold, I am doing a new thing; now it springs forth, do you not perceive it?" (Isaiah 43:19).

HE IS DOING A NEW THING… In your world. In your life. In your job. In your relationships. In your church.

Revival is here. But the question is—do you see it? Do you perceive it? Will you experience it?

Revival isn't just a service you attend. It's not limited to a conference, a tent meeting, or a moment at an altar. Revival is something we all have the ability to carry and experience. As carriers of His presence—it's more than a fleeting moment. It's a lifestyle we are called to embody, a freshness we are mandated to bring into every room we walk into.

But wouldn't it be a tragedy for revival to be poured out at an unprecedented level, and we miss it?

I've seen God pouring out His glory like a great waterfall cascading across the earth. The waters are deep, rushing, and powerful. But to experience it, we must loosen our grip on control.

We must lift our feet in the flood of His power. The question is—will we struggle to keep our footing, or will we surrender and let Him take us deeper?

Revival requires release. It may mean letting go of what was—old places, old spaces, old patterns of thinking, and traditional ways of doing things. I see the Spirit breaking boxes and barriers, shaking foundations to bring forth an unprecedented move of God.

Lord, have Your way. Give us courage and boldness to shoot the arrows You've placed in our hands in this year of double grace.

God is doing something new. Revival is here.
The waters are rising. The Spirit is moving.
Will you step in?

Revival, I hear Revival,
From the depths of who I am.
Nothing else, no one else,
God, only you can.

Take my family, take my goals,
Take every hope and dream.
God, take it ALL.
It's in my surrender that you redeem.

This life is not my own.
God, every part belongs to you,
I release every image,
God do what only you can do.

You made me by your hands,
Created in the depths of a secret place.
To walk and to worship,
At the sound of your amazing grace.

God direct my path,
Every step ordained by you.
Have ALL of me,

Lord, Nothing else will do.

Revival, I hear Revival,
From the depths of who I am.
Nothing else, no one else,
God, only you can.

Don't you understand?
I pray "God give them eyes to see".
It's only His Kingdom that will last,
It's only Jesus that can set you free.

Please, please, please,
Wake up to the reality,
This world is but a breath
Compared to the light of eternity.

What is your house built upon?
Is it the American Dream?
Trying to prove yourself worthy,
Looking at society for esteem.

Release it all to Him,
God will take every part.
Make nothing higher in your life,
Let him reign as King over your heart.

Revival, I hear Revival,
From the depths of who I am.
Nothing else, no one else,
God, only you can.
Declaration Over You:

I declare that your eyes will see and your ears will hear the new thing God is doing.
I declare that you will not miss the outpouring of His Spirit, but that you will step into the rushing waters of revival. I declare that control will break off, fear will lift, and you will flow with the Spirit into deeper places of His presence.

Revival isn't just around you—it's within you. And it is springing forth NOW.

November

Mellonie Baldwin

Meet Mellonie Baldwin

"Charm is deceitful and beauty is vain, but a woman who fears the Lord is to be praised" (Proverbs 31:30). This scripture powerfully reflects the life and calling of Mellonie Elizabeth Baldwin—a true woman of virtue whose identity is deeply rooted in her reverence for God. Her strength does not come from worldly achievements but from her intimate walk with the Lord. As a beloved daughter of the Most High King, Mellonie carries a profound love for God's people and a steadfast commitment to their healing, restoration, and spiritual transformation.

Mellonie is a licensed and ordained Deacon and minister whose greatest earthly joy is her family and her service to the Body of Christ. She is called to lead the broken, the rejected, and the wounded into the arms of Christ where true healing is found. A graduate of Ashland Theological Seminary with a Master's Degree in Pastoral Counseling, Mellonie combines clinical expertise with prophetic insight and spiritual discernment to bring inner healing and deliverance to those she serves. As a Certified Life Coach, she mentors individuals worldwide to walk boldly and authentically in their God-given identity, thrive in kingdom finances, and fulfill their divine purpose to glorify God.

In 2004, under the leading of the Holy Spirit, Mellonie founded Achor Counseling & Associates—a ministry birthed from the heart of God to bring hope to the hurting. Inspired by Hosea 2:14–15, Mellonie stands on the promise that God is turning the "Valley of Trouble" into a doorway of hope for those bound by trauma, shame, abandonment, divorce, and rejection. Her mission is not merely therapeutic—it is deeply spiritual. She ministers from the well of her own testimony, pointing every soul to the only One who heals completely—Jesus Christ.

Since 2012, Mellonie has faithfully served as ordained clergy and remains a Texas Licensed Professional Counselor with extensive experience in integrating biblical truth, inner healing, and clinical wisdom. She passionately believes that healing is available, wholeness is attainable, and purpose is predestined by God. Her life's assignment is to restore identity, awaken purpose, and empower individuals to live healed, free, and on fire for the Kingdom of God.

Beyond counseling and ministry, Mellonie is a visionary entrepreneur and graduate of Capitol One's Getting Down to Business Program, through which she champions financial literacy for women and girls. She is the founder of Absolutely Radiant, a coaching and mentoring movement designed to raise up women who will live fearlessly, shine with the glory of God, and turn the world upside down for Christ.

Mellonie proudly serves under the spiritual covering of Apostle Elaine Benson of Oil of Joy Ministries, where she continues to grow, serve, and be a vessel of apostolic and prophetic transformation.

Mellonie Baldwin is a warrior for souls, a midwife of destiny, and a radiant example of a woman who fears the Lord—worthy of honor, influence, and praise.

The Power of Intercession and Tears

"Weeping may tarry for the night, but joy comes with the morning."
- Psalm 30:5b (ESV)

"Let the priests, who minister before the LORD, weep between the portico and the altar." -Joel 2:17a (NIV)

Devotional Thought

I have witnessed the grace and hand of God move miraculously time and time again. One of the most unforgettable moments was when my nephew stood at death's doorstep, stricken with sepsis. The doctors gave little hope, and we braced ourselves for the worst. Yet, during fear and uncertainty, prayers went up like incense. Believers lifted their voices near and far and against all odds, he was healed.

It was God's grace and the prayers of the righteous that made all the difference. In that moment, I was reminded that prayer is not a ritual, it is life itself.

Prayer is our secret weapon and not just words spoken into the air; it is sacred communion and communication with the living God. It is the place where we lay down burdens too heavy for us to carry, and in exchange, receive His peace, protection, provision, and his unfailing love.

In Matthew chapter seven, Jesus gives us a beautiful invitation: ask, seek, and knock. This is not the invitation of a distant God, but our loving Father who delights in responding to His children with generosity, wisdom, and perfect timing. I believe one of the most powerful forms of prayer is intercession, when we stand in the gap for someone else. Joel 2:17 paints a striking image of priests weeping before the Lord on behalf of the people.

Intercession is not always easy; it costs us time, focus, and sometimes even tears. Don't give up. In those tears, we reflect Christ Himself, our great intercessor, who continually carries our burdens before the Father.

The truth is that tears shed in prayer are never wasted. They water the soil of our faith. They express the groanings of our hearts when words fail us. Psalm 30:5 assures us that while weeping may endure for a night, joy is certain to come in the morning. Every tear is like a seed planted in the dark, destined to bloom into breakthrough, healing, or fresh joy. God bottles every tear, treasures every cry, and turns them into instruments of compassion and power.

When intercession is mingled with tears, heaven responds. These prayers humble us, keep us dependent on God, and draw us closer to His heart. Our enemy trembles when believers pray with persistence and passion because such prayers release the power of heaven into the earth.

So, don't hold back your tears or minimize the power of your prayers. Keep asking. Keep seeking, knocking and interceding with confidence. The night may feel long, but it is not forever. Sometimes the night seems so long, you may find yourself not wanting to pray or prayer has become routine. I encourage you to get back up again and let the fire of God, rekindle your prayer and faith life. Morning is coming, and with it comes joy, healing, and the unmistakable presence of God.

Prayer:
Father, teach me to carry others before You with love and perseverance. Remind me that my tears are precious to You and that none are wasted. Strengthen my faith to keep pressing in until Your joy, healing, and breakthrough come forth. In Jesus' name, Amen.

Declarations:
I declare that my tears are not wasted but are seeds of joy and breakthrough. I declare that I am a faithful intercessor, standing in the gap for others. I declare that heaven responds when I cry out with persistence and passion.

Reflection:
Who is God placing on my heart to intercede for today? Where am I believing God to turn my weeping into joy?

Multiplied Authority: The Power of Agreement

Scripture Focus

"Again I say to you, if two of you agree on earth about anything they ask, it will be done for them by my Father in heaven. For where two or three gather in my name, there am I with them." Matthew 18:19–20

"When Mordecai learned of all that had been done, he tore his clothes, put on sackcloth and ashes, and went out into the city, wailing loudly and bitterly." Esther 4:1–3

Devotional Thought

I am honored to have been chosen to be a part of Women of Valor as an intercessor and writing contributor. The mission of WOV, has always been in line with God's fulfillment of His kingdom and the great commission.

How powerful the body of Christ could be, if we came into agreement. A red wave, and I am speaking of, the blood of Jesus. Unity will only come when we come under his banner.
What if believers of all denominations came together for one cause, building up the kingdom of God. What if we truly loved one another and gave up our individual or denominational agendas.

Jesus Himself assures us that "where two or three gather in my name, there am I with them" (Matthew 18:20). This means, there is power in agreement when unity in prayer, is not just religious practice. It is heaven's strategy for breakthrough.

When God's people come together with one heart and one voice, the atmosphere shifts, darkness is pushed back, and chains are broken. God's power is released in ways far greater, than what one person could accomplish alone.

The story of Esther paints this truth vividly. Faced with the annihilation of her people, Esther could not afford to act alone. Mordecai called the Jewish people to fast and pray in unity, and Esther herself relied not on her royal position but on the intercession of her community. Their united prayers turned the tide of history. What was planned for their destruction became a divine reversal, a testimony of God's saving power.

I have seen this kind of breakthrough personally. During a family crisis, my prayers felt heavy, and at times I didn't have the strength to keep believing. But when my family, my WOV sisters and my church family prayed with and for me, something shifted.

Their faith strengthened mine, and together we called on heaven. It didn't happen overnight, but I watched God move in ways I could never have orchestrated. That experience reminded me that agreement multiplies strength. Prayer is not our last resort; it is God's first strategy.

This shows us that there are some battles we cannot fight alone. Personal prayer is powerful, but corporate prayer carries a multiplied authority that shakes the kingdom of darkness. When we choose unity over isolation and prayer over panic, we make space for God to do the miraculous.

Now more than ever, we are called to be watchmen and intercessors for the world. And often, the joy of the morning is borne through the prayers of the night. I salute all the watchmen on the wall.

Prayer

Father, thank You for the gift of unity and the power of agreement. Teach us to stand together in prayer with boldness, humility, and faith. Help us to rise in this generation, interceding with courage and trusting You for divine reversal. In Jesus' name, Amen.
• I declare that united prayer releases supernatural power and divine breakthrough.
• I declare that my prayers, combined with others, disrupt the plans of the enemy.

Reflection Questions

1. Is there an area where you've been carrying the battle alone but need to invite others into prayer with you?

2. Like Mordecai or Esther, what role is God calling you to play in intercession for your family, church, or nation?

3. How does knowing that God can bring divine reversal encourage you to pray with greater persistence?

December

Brunell Johnson

Meet Brunell Johnson

Apostle Brunell Johnson (God's Girl) is a native Houstonian currently residing in the Cypress area. She's the proud wife of Overseer Larry Johnson. A mother and grandmother. Family & living a balanced life is very important to her. Brunell accepted Jesus Christ as her Lord and Savior as a child at an early age. She is a licensed Minister-Evangelist through the Church of God in Christ organization. She also has a Bachelor of Science in Ministry from Vision International. She is a Certified Christian Counselor, and a Certified Life Coach. She is A Philanthropist, providing financial assistance, meals for the elderly and many in need. She also helps to supply clothing and other necessities to families who struggle to meet their basic needs.

Apostle Brunell is the proud Pastor and founder of House of Restoration Worship Center Church in Houston, TX. She purposes herself to live her life with the Holy bible as her foundation. She lives the life that she preaches, teaches and dances about. Her desire is to please God in every area of her life. She is passionate about God's people and the ministry that God has placed within her. Apostle Brunell wants the ministry she has been entrusted with to bring about healing, deliverance and empowerment to the people of God. She understands that she has been Empowered to Empower and Transformed to Transform. She believes that a relationship with the Trinity is essential for living a successful life.

Apostle Brunell is a Proud board member of Women of Valour founded by Dr. Allison Wiley. She is a Co-Author of a book of Inspirational writing with her WOV sisters. She writes plays and skits to inspire and empower. She has led an Intercessory Ministry for the past 7 years that has taken up the mantle of pray for many people, nations, and causes at 6:30AM, Monday – Friday without fail and have witness the miraculous power of God by way of answered prayers. Being a Victor over sexual & physical abuse, she helps Women and Young girls who have been abused overcome the effects of their abuse to live healthy and whole lives.

Apostle Brunell has appeared on many radio broadcasts spreading the word of God. She is an International Speaker reaching many in Kenya, Ghana, Nigeria, South Africa, Pakistan, Zimbabwe, London, and many more countries. Apostle Brunell states that when she leaves this earth, she wants to be an empty vessel that God used to the fullest.

God Has Graced You To Finish Strong

"Better is the end of a thing than its beginning; and the patient in spirit is better than the proud in spirit."
- Ecclesiastes 7:8

This passage reminds us that perseverance and patience are essential to completing what we start. While challenges and setbacks may arise, intentionality and determination enable us to overcome obstacles and achieve our goals.

As we enter the final month of 2025, reflect on your journey, celebrate your achievements, learn from your difficulties, and recognize the grace that has carried you this far. We are in December, the twelfth month, and we know that the number 12 symbolizes God's divine order, authority and completeness. The number 25 represents grace and redemption. Therefore, signifying an opportunity to finish the year with renewed strength and purpose.

Take time to evaluate what needs to be released or adjusted in your life to ensure alignment with our heavenly Father, values and faith. Equip yourself with resilience, discipline, and wise counsel to move forward confidently.

Do not be discouraged by delays, disappointments, or setbacks. Instead, use these experiences as motivation to pursue your purpose. Remember, setbacks are preparation for future victories. As Proverbs 24:16 says, "A just person falls seven times and rises again." You have the strength and grace to finish strong.

Prayer:
Lord, bless those who read this message. May they recognize Your guidance and purpose in every circumstance. Thank You for granting them the grace to finish strong. In Jesus name, Amen.

Declaration:
I will finish strong!
My past will not define or stop me!
I have been graced to finish strong.

Unshakable Faith
Daniel 3:12-30

Hananiah (Shadrach), Mishael (Meshach), and Azariah (Abednego) were men of unwavering faith, tremendous courage, and honor towards God. Their devotion was not limited to moments of comfort or ease; it remained steadfast even when they were confronted with the threat of death in a fiery furnace. Through every test and trial, they continued to trust God. They chose to obey God's word, believing that, regardless of the consequences of disobeying human authority, God would protect them.

The decree was issued requiring everyone to bow at the sound of the music, but they stood their ground. They boldly declared to the King, that under no circumstances, would they worship any god except their own. The king became furious, ordered the furnace to be heated seven times hotter than usual and commanded that Shadrach, Meshach, and Abednego be thrown into it. The men tasked with casting them into the flames were consumed by the fire, while Shadrach, Meshach, and Abednego were walking around free and completely unharmed.

Witnessing this miracle, the king was astonished and said to his counselors, "Didn't we throw in three men bound? But I see four walking freely, unharmed, and the fourth looks like the son of the gods." The king called the men out of the fire, and not only were they unharmed, but they did look like what they had been through. In response, the king issued a decree that anyone who spoke against the true and living God would be punished severely, and he elevated Shadrach, Meshach, and Abednego to positions of honor.

The moral of this story is clear: stand your ground and believe in God beyond what you see, feel, or hear. Trust that God is working behind the scenes to bring you victory. Be intentional in your actions and walk by faith, not by sight, knowing that you can walk through the fire and emerge without smelling like smoke.

Prayer: Lord, help me to have unshakeable faith and always trust you, in Jesus' name, amen.

Declaration: I am not moved by what I see! I have unshakeable faith!

Made in the USA
Coppell, TX
08 February 2026

70578600R10085